Use It!
Reuse It!

Wood

Dana Meachen Rau

mc **Marshall Cavendish**
Benchmark
New York

Other Marshall Cavendish Offices:
Marshall Cavendish International (Asia) Private Limited, 1 New Industrial Road, Singapore 536196 • Marshall Cavendish International (Thailand) Co Ltd. 253 Asoke, 12th Flr, Sukhumvit 21 Road, Klongtoey Nua, Wattana, Bangkok 10110, Thailand • Marshall Cavendish (Malaysia) Sdn Bhd, Times Subang, Lot 46, Subang Hi-Tech Industrial Park, Batu Tiga, 40000 Shah Alam, Selangor Darul Ehsan, Malaysia

Marshall Cavendish is a trademark of Times Publishing Limited.

All websites were available and accurate when this book was sent to press.

Editor: Christina Gardeski
Publisher: Michelle Bisson
Art Director: Anahid Hamparian
Series Designer: Virginia Pope

Printed in Malaysia
1 3 5 6 4 2

Library of Congress Cataloging-in-Publication Data
Rau, Dana Meachen, 1971–
Wood / Dana Meachen Rau.
pages cm. — (Use It! Reuse It!)
Includes bibliographical references and index.
Summary: "Examines how we use wood in everyday objects, its unique traits and qualities, and how it is processed to be useful to us. Also discusses how wood can be recycled to use again"—Provided by publisher.
ISBN 978-1-60870-519-1 (print)
ISBN 978-1-60870-775-1 (ebook)
1. Wood—Juvenile literature. I. Title.
TA419.R23 2011
620.1'2—dc22
2010050196

Photo research by Connie Gardner

Cover photo by Imagebroker/Superstock

The photographs in this book are used by permission and through the courtesy of: *Alamy*: p. 3 Elizabeth Whiting and Associates; p. 5(R) Imagebroker; p. 13(T) Paris Pierce; p. 13(B) Jack Sullivan; p. 21(T) Stock Asylum. *Getty Images*: p. 4 Stone; p. 5(C) Workbook Stock; p. 5(L) David Prince; p. 10(R) MPL Stringer; p. 21(B) Bambu Productions. *Superstock*: p. 6(L) Dwight Elletesen; p. 6(R) age fotostock; p. 7(B) Chris Pearsall; p. 9(T) Newberry Library; p. 12(R) Roy Kino; p. 14 F1 Online; p. 15 Photononstop; p. 17 Imagebroker. *The Image Works*: p. 7(T) Rob Crandall; p. 16(T) David R. Frazier; pp. 1, 16(B) Bob Daemmrich; p. 16(C) Adam Tanner. *Corbis*: p. 8 Bettmann; p. 19 Ariel Skelley; p. 20(L) Richard Hamilton Smith; p. 20(R) Encyclopedia. *Art Resource*: p. 9(L) The Newark Museum; p. 9(B) SSPL/Science Museum; p. 11 The New York Public Library; p. 10(L) Werner Forman; p. 12(L) Bildarchive Preusaischer Kulturbesitz. *AP Photo*: p. 18.

Wood

Chapter 1

A builder uses wood to make the framework of a house.

Wood from the Woods

Forests are full of trees. Trees are made of wood. But you don't have to go to a forest to see wood. Wood is all around us.

Open the door. Run up the stairs. Sit in a chair. All of these things may be made of wood. People use wood to build houses, bridges, boats, fences, floors, playground equipment, and more!

Wood can be cut and **carved** into shapes. So it is used to make furniture, broom handles, and toys. You may write with a wooden pencil or play with a wooden baseball bat. Maybe you like licking a frozen treat on a wooden stick, or making music on a wooden xylophone.

Wood helps you enter a house, play a game, or hold a treat!

If a tree loses its leaves in the fall, it's a broadleaf (left). Most conifer trees stay green all year.

The two main kinds of trees are **broadleaf** and **conifer**. Oak and maple are types of broadleaf trees. These trees lose their leaves in the fall. Conifer trees often have long, thin leaves that look like needles. They also grow cones. Most conifers stay green all year long. Redwood and hemlock are types of conifers.

Wood comes from the trunk, or stem, of the tree. The main job of the strong center trunk is to hold up the tree's branches and bring water and **nutrients** up from the underground roots. The leaves on the branches take in energy from the sun. The tree uses this energy to make food. This food travels down the trunk to the roots. The bark on the trunk protects the tree. As the tree gets older, the trunk grows wider, adding a ring of wood each year.

People cut down trees to use their wood to make huge buildings and tiny toothpicks. Inside, outside, on your desk, or on a roller coaster— you can find wood everywhere you go.

The branches of trees reach high into the sky. Their roots grow deep underground.

leaves

branches

trunk (or stem)

roots

Inside a trunk, you can see its rings. A tree grows a new ring every year.

Chapter 2

Strong teams of horses were needed to pull heavy logs to the sawmill.

The Story of Logging

Long ago, the earliest people burned wood to make fire. They used tree branches to make **shelters**. They carved wood into sculptures and tools.

With axes, people cut down all the trees in an area to use the land for growing crops. They carved wood for furniture at home, tools for work, and toys for play.

Some American Indian groups used wooden branches to hold up their shelters.

Wood was a strong material, good for items people used a lot, such as furniture and toys.

9

The Vikings traveled the seas in ships built of wood.

Two people had to work together to cut a tree with a crosscut saw. This type of saw had two handles.

They cut wood into **lumber**. They could use these boards to make homes and buildings.

Explorers and **merchants** needed wood, too. Large wooden ships sailed across oceans. Small canoes traveled the rivers and streams. Wooden carts and wagons rolled on wooden wheels. Wooden sleds carried people across cold, icy land and frozen waterways.

When settlers came to America in the 1600s, **logging** became an important job. Loggers set up camps in the woods near rivers. A camp had cabins for workers to sleep and eat. A barn held their animals. Life was rough and dangerous in a logging camp.

The loggers worked all day **felling** trees with axes and saws. Horses and oxen dragged the logs to the river. The loggers tied the logs together into rafts and floated them to a **sawmill**, where the logs were cut into lumber.

Loggers set up camps in the forest where they worked. They lived in these camps during the whole cutting season.

From the sawmill, lumber was sold to people to make things. A cooper made barrels. A shipwright made ships. A wheelwright made wheels. These woodworkers could bend, carve, or shape the wood.

Over time, new tools and machines made logging easier. More loggers used saws, which cut wood faster than axes. In the 1800s, **steam** was a new way to power machines for cutting. Railroads could

Coopers used lumber to make barrels. Wheelwrights were skilled at turning wood into wheels for carts and wagons (right).

Steam trains carried logs long distances from forest to sawmill.

move heavy logs if there was no river nearby. Gas-powered chainsaws, invented in 1929, helped loggers fell trees faster. Today, loggers and mills use modern tools and machines to fell trees, cut lumber, and make products. But like long ago, logging is still a dangerous job!

Logging can be dangerous. This logger wears special gear for protection.

Chapter 3

Electric saws help loggers make clean cuts through huge logs.

Turning Trees into Lumber

Today, loggers fell trees with powerful saws and big machines that can grab, saw, and pick them up. Loggers can cut trees to fall safely so no people, machines, or other trees are in their way.

Next, they saw off the branches and cut the trunk into smaller pieces. Large machines that can handle heavy loads drag or pick up the logs. Logs travel by river, train, or truck to the sawmill.

Powerful machines help load a truck headed for the sawmill.

At the sawmill, a machine takes all of the bark off the logs. A **head saw** passes through the log. This saw cuts back and forth along the log, sawing it into boards. The boards move on to another set of saws that make the edges straight and trim the ends.

Before the lumber can be made into buildings or products, it has to be **seasoned**. Wood holds water, so the sawmill may let the lumber dry out in the sun or put the boards through a heated **kiln**. When a board dries, it shrinks and may even bend a little. After the wood is seasoned, it is ready to send to a lumberyard or home store to be sold to companies or woodworkers.

First, logs are stripped of their bark (top). Next, the log is cut into boards (above). These boards (below) are ready to use.

If a piece of lumber is cut from the center of a tree, the lines of the wood will be straight. If it is cut along the edges, it will have a curvier grain.

No two trees grow in exactly the same way. So each piece of lumber is a little different, too. You may see straight or curvy lines on a piece of wood. This **wood grain** is the lines made by the rings of the tree. Dark, round spots are called **knots**. The knots are places where branches once grew from the trunk. Wood also has different colors depending on the tree it came from, like white, yellow, or even red.

A product made of wood doesn't look like a tree anymore. But you can see clues that it was once a tree by its patterns and colors.

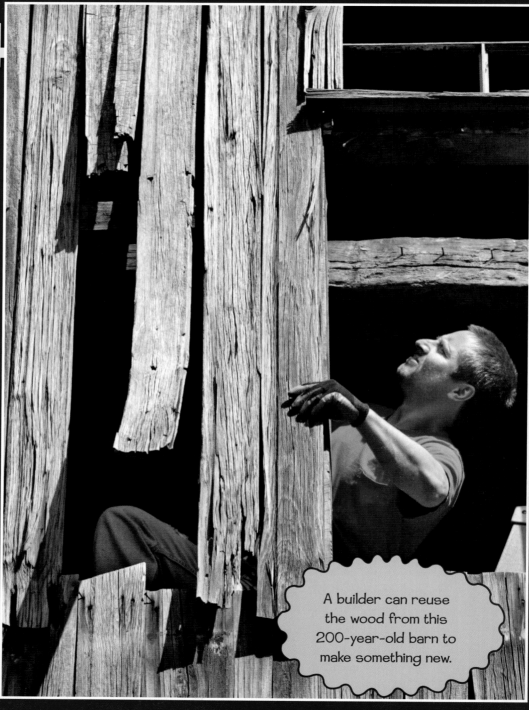

Chapter 4

A builder can reuse the wood from this 200-year-old barn to make something new.

Reusing Wood

Trees take a long time to grow big—sometimes hundreds of years! So when loggers choose the best trees to cut, they make sure plenty of trees are still growing. It is good to reuse wood, too, so we don't cut down any more trees than we have to.

If an old barn is falling apart or no longer used, a builder might use some of its wood to build something else. The barn boards can be used to make a floor for a new home, office, or store.

You don't need to throw away an old chair! Refinish it with new stain or paint.

Old furniture can be used again, too. Some people look for furniture at tag sales. They **refinish** it by fixing it up to look like new.

Wood chips from the sawmill can decorate the ground in a garden.

At this construction site, builders set aside wood that can be used again.

Sawmills not only make lumber. They also make a lot of sawdust and wood chips! These can be made into paper, fuel, or other wood products. Wood chips can also be used to cover the ground in a garden and keep out weeds.

If you like working with wood, you don't have to cut down a tree. You can often get scraps of lumber from a lumberyard or construction site. You can take apart an old crate and use its boards. Make sure you are safe when working with wood. Use the right tools and always work with an adult.

Start by building something small, like a birdhouse. Try making a pair of stilts. You may even be able to build a tree house!

A wooden tree house in a tree? You would truly have wood all around you!

Small scraps of wood are perfect for a birdhouse.

Make a shelter for yourself high in a tree with wood!

21

Glossary

broadleaf [BRAWD-leef] trees that lose their leaves in the fall

carved [KAHRVD] shaped by cutting

conifer [KAH-nuh-fer] trees with needles and cones that stay green all year

felling [FEL-ing] cutting down trees

head saw [HED SAW] a machine at the sawmill that cuts the log into boards

kiln [KILN] an oven used to dry out wood

knots [NOTS] circle shapes in lumber where branches once grew from the trunk

logging [LAH-ging] the business of cutting down trees to be made into lumber

lumber [LUHM-ber] wooden boards cut from the trunk of a tree

merchants [MUR-chuhnts] people who buy and sell goods

nutrients [NOO-tree-uhnts] food needed to live

refinish [ree-FIN-ish] to make something old look new again by stripping off old paint, sanding it smooth, and painting or staining it again

sawmill [SAW-mil] the place where logs are turned into lumber

seasoned [SEE-zuhnd] dried out

shelters [SHEL-ters] places protected from weather, such as houses

steam [STEEM] water vapor that enters the air from boiling water

wood grain [WOOD GREYN] the lines on a piece of lumber created by the rings of the tree trunk

Books to Discover

Chapman, Gillian. *Making Art with Wood*. New York: PowerKids Press, 2007.

Ditchfield, Christin. *Wood*. New York: Children's Press, 2003.

Jennings, Terry J. *Material Matters: Wood*. N. Mankato, MN: Chrysalis Children's Books, 2003.

Kalman, Bobbie, and Deanna Brady. *Colonial People: The Woodworkers*. New York: Crabtree Publishing, 2002.

Kelsey, John. *Kid Crafts: Woodworking*. East Petersburg, PA: Fox Chapel Publishing, 2008.

Websites to Explore

Arbor Day Foundation
www.arborday.org
The Pennsylvania Lumber Museum
www.lumbermuseum.org
United States Forest Service
www.fs.fed.us
What Tree Is It?
www.oplin.org/tree

Index

Page numbers in **boldface**
are illustrations.

American Indians, **9**
axes, 9, 12

bark, 7, 16, **16**
barn boards, **18**, 19
boards, 16, **16**, 19, 20
boats, 5, 10, **10**
branches, 6, **7**, 9, **9**, 15, 17
broadleaf trees, 6, **6**
builder, **4**, 18, **20**
building materials, **4**, 5, 7, 9, 10, 16, **21**

carving, 5, 9, **9**
chainsaws, 13
colors, 17
conifer trees, 6, **6**
construction site, 20, **20**
cooper, 12, **12**
cropland, 9
crosscut saw, **10**

felling trees, 11, 13, 15, 19, 20
furniture, 9, **9**, 19, **19**

head saw, 16
home store, 16

kiln, 16
knots, 17, **17**

leaves, 6, **6**, **7**, **11**
loggers, 11, **11**, 13, **13**, **14**, 15, 19
logging, 11, 13, **13**
logging camps, 11, **11**
logs, **8**, 13, **13**, **14**, 15, 16, **16**
lumber, 10–13, 16, 17, **17**, 20
lumberyard, 16, 20

machines, 12, 13, 15, **15**
merchants, 10

nutrients, 6

products, **4**, 5, **5**, 16, 17, 20

railroads, 12, **13**
refinish, 19, **19**
reuse, 18, 19, 20
rings, 7, **7**
roots, 6, 7, **7**

sawdust, 20
sawmill, **8**, 11, 12, 13, **13**,
    15, **15**, 16, 20, **20**
saws, **10**, 12, 13, **14**, 15
scraps of wood, 20, **21**
seasoned, 16
settlers, 11
shelters, 9, **9**, **21**
ships, 10, **10**, 12
shipwright, 12
steam power, 12, **13**
sun energy, 6

tools, 9, **10**, 12, 13, **14**, 15, 20–21
transportation, **8**, 10, **10**, 11–13, 15
tree house, 21, **21**
tree parts, 6, 7, **7**
trees, kinds of, 6, **6**
trunk, 6, 7, **7**, 15, 17

Vikings, **10**

wheelwright, 12, **12**
wood characteristics, 5
wood chips, 20, **20**
wood grain, 17, **17**

About the Author

Dana Meachen Rau is the author of more than 250 books for children. She has written about many nonfiction topics from her home office in Burlington, Connecticut. One of Dana's favorite things to do is hike through the woods and admire the trees.

With thanks to the Reading Consultants:

Nanci R. Vargus, Ed.D., is an Assistant Professor of Elementary Education at the University of Indianapolis.

Beth Walker Gambro is an Adjunct Professor at the University of Saint Francis in Joliet, Illinois.